CONSIDERING EVERY SIDE

ANALYZING SITUATIONS

DAVID KLIMCHUK

PowerKiDS press.

NEW YORK

Published in 2020 by The Rosen Publishing Group, Inc.
29 East 21st Street, New York, NY 10010

Editor: Elizabeth Krajnik
Designer: Michael Flynn

Photo Credits: Cover Klaus Vedfelt/DigitalVision/Getty Images; cover, pp. 1, 3–4, 6–8, 10–14, 16, 18, 20, 22–24 (background) TairA/Shutterstock.com; p. 5 Zdravinjo/Shutterstock.com; p. 6 Catalin Petolea/Shutterstock.com; p. 7 Natalia Mels/Shutterstock.com; p. 8 saragosa69/Shutterstock.com; pp. 9, 19 Monkey Business Images/ Shutterstock.com; p. 10 Fresnel/Shutterstock.com; p. 11 Bettmann/Getty Images; p. 12 Rawpixel.com/Shutterstock. com; p. 13 mediaphotos/iStock/Getty Images; p. 15 Bonnie Jo Mount/The Washington Post/Getty Images; p. 16 32 pixels/Shutterstock.com; p. 17 D Dipasupil/Getty Images North America/Getty Images; p. 18 Motortion Films/ Shutterstock.com; p. 20 kak2s/Shutterstock.com; p. 21 Flotsam/Shutterstock.com; p. 22 piotr_pabijan/Shutterstock. com.

Library of Congress Cataloging-in-Publication Data

Names: Klimchuk, David, author.
Title: Considering every side : analyzing situations / David Klimchuk.
Description: New York : PowerKids Press, [2020] | Series: Spotlight on social
  and emotional learning | Series: Spotlight on social and emotional
  learning | Includes index.
Identifiers: LCCN 2019005180| ISBN 9781725306646 (pbk.) | ISBN 9781725306677
  (library bound) | ISBN 9781725306653 (6 pack)
Subjects: LCSH: Judgment in children--Juvenile literature. | Decision making
  in children--Juvenile literature.
Classification: LCC BF723.J8 K585 2020 | DDC 155.4/1383--dc23
LC record available at https://lccn.loc.gov/2019005180

Manufactured in the United States of America

CPSIA Compliance Information: Batch #CWPK20. For further information contact Rosen Publishing, New York, New York at 1-800-237-9932.

CONTENTS

CHAPTER ONE

STUDYING THE SITUATION

Every day, people run into different situations that challenge them in big and small ways. It can be easy for people to jump into these situations without thinking and to do something they **regret**. That's why analyzing the situation first can be very useful. If people don't have all the facts, they might judge a person or idea unfairly. To analyze something means to study and examine it very carefully to see more clearly what's going on.

Analyzing situations also helps us learn what people, ideas, or suggestions they can trust and which ones need more **investigating**. For example, if one of your friends tells you that cheating on a test could help you get a better grade, you might want to analyze how much you can trust that person and what the consequences could be.

Sometimes conflict or arguments can be avoided by taking time to analyze a situation before acting.

CHAPTER TWO

MAKING GOOD CHOICES

Analyzing situations is an important social and emotional learning skill that helps people make responsible decisions. Many times, people **respond** to challenging situations with emotions such as anger, sadness, or guilt. These emotions might cause people to act quickly and irresponsibly without thinking more about it. This can cause a big mess! If people stop and think about the different parts of the situation, they can deal with the emotions and respond **appropriately**. They might even find that the situation isn't as bad as they thought and their feelings might change.

Analyzing situations can help people make good choices, such as choosing healthy foods over unhealthy foods.

Sometimes unexpected situations happen, and people have to adapt, or change, to handle them. By learning and practicing skills for analyzing situations, people may find they get along better with others and feel more **confident**.

CHAPTER THREE

WHAT'S THE PROBLEM?

The ability to analyze situations is a very useful skill. For example, your friend may want you to come over after school, but you know you have homework to do. You may need to analyze the situation before making a decision too quickly.

Before you start analyzing, it's helpful to stop and think about what exactly the problem is. This will help you make the best choice **efficiently**. In the example above, the problem is that you can't do homework and play at the same time. By the end of the day, your homework must be done, or you may get in trouble or get a bad grade. Your problem will be solved if you decide to do homework before playing with your friend. However, if you don't know what the problem is, you might act on your emotions and decide to play instead of doing your homework.

Moving too quickly when you have a decision to make can lead to mistakes.

CHAPTER FOUR

LOOKING INTO IT

The next step in analyzing a situation is to spend time looking into what's going on. This means asking questions so you have more **information** and can make the best choices. By getting more information and noticing different parts of the situation, you can be better prepared to tackle whatever's in front of you.

Abraham Maslow, an American **psychologist**, came up with the idea of a **hierarchy** of needs, which breaks down our needs based on what's most needed for us to survive.

One important question to ask is: "What do I actually *need*?" Sometimes people act on something they *want*, which doesn't always help them. Separating needs from wants can save people a lot of trouble. Another question is: "How will this affect other people?" When people's emotions take over, they sometimes only think about how the outcome of a situation will affect them, not how it will affect anyone else. Before making any decisions, try asking some of these questions.

CHAPTER FIVE

DIFFERENT SIDES TO THE STORY

No two people are exactly the same. Everyone has their own experiences that make them special and one of a kind. When analyzing a situation, it's important to remember that different people might have very different **perspectives**. For example, if your teacher asks your class to write down all the words that come to mind when they think of the word "neighborhood," everyone would have different responses. This is because everyone has their own idea of what a neighborhood may look, smell, sound, or feel like. The same thing applies to how people see different situations.

Alex F. Osborn, an American businessman and author, came up with the idea of brainstorming, which is when a group tries to solve a problem by coming up with a number of different ideas at the same time and writing them down.

BRAINSTORM

One way to practice seeing different sides of the story is to ask yourself, "How would I feel if I were the other person?" This question can help you be more empathetic, or understanding of and able to share other people's emotions and experiences.

CHAPTER SIX

WHAT CAN YOU CONTROL?

An important part of analyzing situations is knowing what can and what can't be controlled. One way to work through unpleasant situations is to learn how to balance what can be changed and what needs to be accepted. Sometimes there are parts of a situation that people can't change.

For example, you can't make your teacher stop giving your class homework just because you don't want to do it. When analyzing this situation, you may realize that you can't control your teacher's choices. The teacher is in charge and needs to be respected. However, something you can control is how you respond to the situation. If you're having a hard time understanding the homework, you can ask the teacher, your parents, or a classmate for help. Knowing what can be changed and what needs to be accepted can help people make more responsible decisions.

Tara Brach, an American psychologist, is well known for teaching people how to be more accepting of themselves, others, and the situations they experience.

CHAPTER SEVEN

STOP AND THINK

It's much easier to analyze a situation if you stop and think before acting on your emotions. One way to do this is to use the STOP skill.

The "S" stands for "stop." Don't move. Don't say anything. Just stop in your tracks! The "T" stands for "take a step back." This means to actually step back or to at least try to emotionally take yourself out of the situation so you can see everything clearly. The "O" stands for "observe." Observe your thoughts and feelings, the body language of the person you're talking to, and the other people, places, and things around you. The "P" stands for "proceed mindfully." In this step, you act wisely, reasonably, and gently instead of emotionally and without thinking. This skill helps people think about the whole situation fairly.

Jon Kabat-Zinn is an American scientist and author. He has written a number of books on mindfulness. Mindfulness is a key part of the STOP skill.

CHAPTER EIGHT

WHAT'S YOUR GOAL?

It's hard to analyze situations and make responsible decisions if you don't know what your goal is. Without some direction, the chances you'll be able to **effectively** analyze the situation goes down.

It's helpful to ask yourself, "What do I want to get out of this situation?" The answer to this question may make what's happening and what you need to do clearer. For example, if a bully tries to pick on you or your friends at school, having a clear goal could affect or change the outcome. You might want to fight back or to hurt them in some way. However, if your goal is to keep everyone safe, this might not be the best choice. Another choice might be to get away from the bully and tell a teacher.

Writing down your goals can help you effectively analyze a situation.

CHAPTER NINE

MAKING A SMART DECISION

After identifying the problem, setting a goal, and seeing the situation from other perspectives, the next step in analyzing situations is to come up with ways to solve the problem and make a smart decision. You and people you trust, such as your friends, your parents, or other trusted adults, could brainstorm to find a solution.

When you brainstorm, you should think about all you know so far about the situation and come up with a list of things you could do to solve the problem. For example, if you're thinking about ways to deal with a friend who is sad, your brainstorming list might look like this:

CHOICE 1: Do nothing.

CHOICE 2: Ask them what's wrong and try to help them feel better.

CHOICE 3: Tell a teacher who might be able to call your friend's parents.

Taking time to think things through can help you come up with more than one choice so you can make a smart decision.

CHAPTER TEN

TOOLS FOR DECISION MAKING

Analyzing situations is a helpful way to make good decisions. Here are a few other tools for problem solving and responsible decision making.

One helpful tool is making a pros and cons list. On one half of a sheet of paper, write down all the possible good outcomes from making a decision. On the other half of the sheet of paper, write down all the bad outcomes from making that decision. After you're done, look at both sides and weigh what's most important. It may be helpful to ask other people for their thoughts about the situation. A friend, parent, or teacher might be able to give you ideas that are more reasonable because they aren't in the situation. The last tool for decision making might be learning more about effective solutions. Whatever tools you use to make decisions, just make sure you're looking at all sides!

PROS | CONS

GLOSSARY

appropriately (uh-PROH-pree-uht-lee) Done in a way that is right or suited for some purpose or situation.

confident (KAHN-fuh-duhnt) Feeling that you can do something well.

effectively (ih-FEHK-tiv-lee) Done in a way that produces a wanted result.

efficiently (ih-FIH-shuhnt-lee) Done in a way that's capable of bringing about a wanted result without wasting materials, time, or energy.

hierarchy (HI-uh-rahr-kee) A system in which people or things are organized in a series of levels with different importance or status.

information (ihn-fuhr-MAY-shuhn) Knowledge or facts about something.

investigate (ihn-VEH-stuh-gayt) To look at or closely study something to get information about it.

perspective (puhr-SPEHK-tihv) Point of view.

psychologist (si-KAH-luh-jihst) A person who studies psychology, or the science or study of the mind and behavior.

regret (rih-GREHT) To feel sad or sorry about something that you did or didn't do.

respond (rih-SPAHND) To do something as a reaction to something that has happened or been done.

INDEX

PRIMARY SOURCE LIST

Page 11
Abraham Harold Maslow, Psychologist. Photograph. Now kept in the Bettmann collection on Getty Images.

Page 15
Tara Brach speaks at River Road Unitarian Church in Bethesda, MD. Photograph. Bonnie Jo Mount. February 6, 2013. Now kept in the *Washington Post* collection on Getty Images.

Page 17
Jon Kabat-Zinn attends THRIVE: A Third Metric Live Event at New York City Center. Photograph. D Dipasupil. April 25, 2014. Now kept in the Getty Images Entertainment collection on Getty Images.

WEBSITES

Due to the changing nature of Internet links, PowerKids Press has developed an online list of websites related to the subject of this book. This site is updated regularly. Please use this link to access the list: www.powerkidslinks.com/SSEL/analyzing